Golf, Golf, Golf

Golf, Golf, Golf

A Hilarious Collection
of Cartoons

Edited by S. Gross

BARNES
&NOBLE
B O O K S
NEW YORK

To Irv and Ellie—a couple of golf nuts

Copyright © 1989 by S. Gross

This edition published by Barnes & Noble, Inc.,
by arrangement with Sam Gross

1999 Barnes & Noble Books

ISBN 0-7607-1181-X *casebound*
ISBN 0-7607-1182-8 *paperback*

Grateful acknowledgment is made for permission to reprint the
following:

Cartoon on page 124 by Donald Reilly in *Playboy*. Copyright © 1983
by *Playboy*. Reproduced by special permission of *Playboy* magazine.

Cartoons copyrighted by *The New Yorker* are indicated throughout
the book.

Some of the cartoons in this collection have appeared in the following
periodicals and are reprinted by permission of the authors: *Diversion,
El Mundo, Family Circle, Fore, Friends Magazine, Golf Digest, Good
Housekeeping, Parade, Plain Dealer, Saturday Evening Post, Scouting.*

Printed and bound in Mexico

    01 02 03 MC 9 8 7 6 5 4 3
00 01 02 03 MP 9 8 7 6 5 4 3 2 1

RRD-RE

"You're going to shoot
a hundred and fourteen, dear."

JERRY MARCUS

3

4

LO LINKERT

OLIVER CHRISTIANSON (REVILO)

5

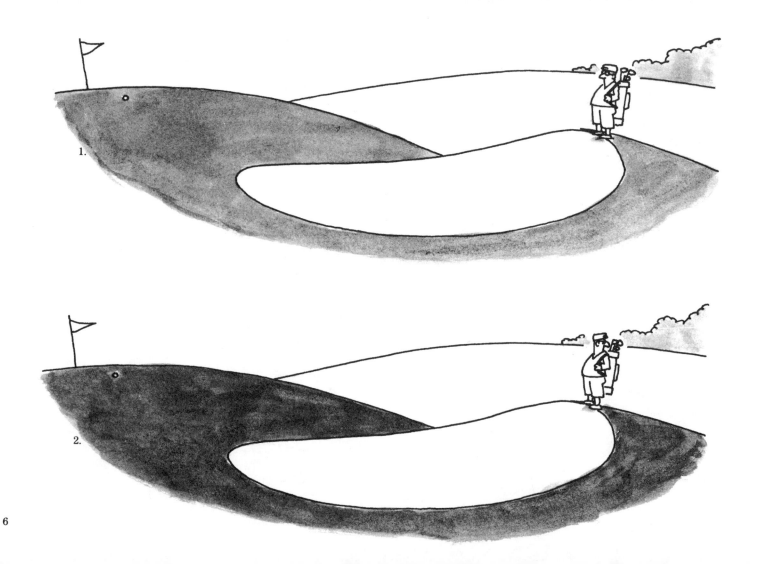

1.

2.

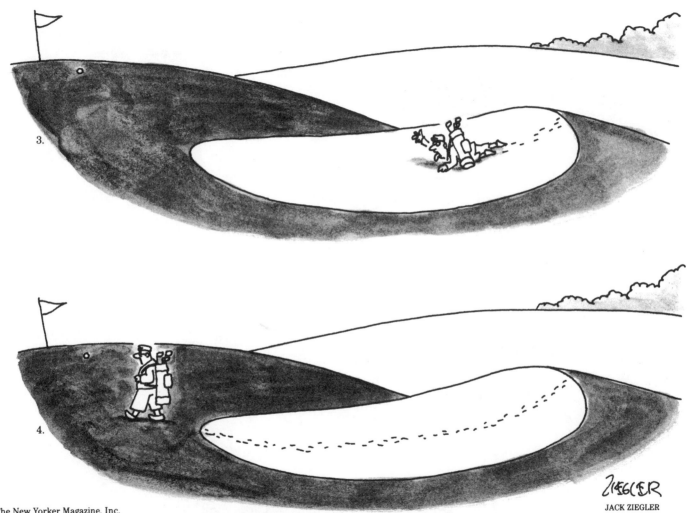

3.

4.

JACK ZIEGLER

"Your grip is okay, but your stance is a little wide."

"Chip's feet were cold."

9

"He's not having a good day. He shot his age this morning."

JOHN JONIK

"Be careful of that grass trap, Akim."

NICK DOWNES

ED FRASCINO

"I'll let you know where to send the rest of my things."

DICK OLDDEN

JOHN JONIK

13

LO LINKERT

"Teeing off early?"

14

In search of the missing links.

MICHAEL MASLIN

15

ORLANDO BUSINO

"I don't know, 'fore' hardly seems adequate."

17

18

"Believe me, when we get back, I'm going to have a word with
the Green's Committee!"

BILL WOODMAN

19

"I wasn't talking to you. I was talking to my nine iron."

ED FRASCINO

JONIK

JOHN JONIK

ELDON DEDINI

CONDOMS FOR GOLFERS

23

"Mr. Sammett's caddie just called to say he's stuck in a sand trap on the ninth green."

MIKE TWOHY

24

"Nasty slice you've got there!"

25

FELIPE GALINDO (FEGGO)

"Every day they get a new hazard on this course."

ORLANDO BUSINO

27

David slew Goliath with a great "swing," not "sling," as previously reported.

JOHN JONIK

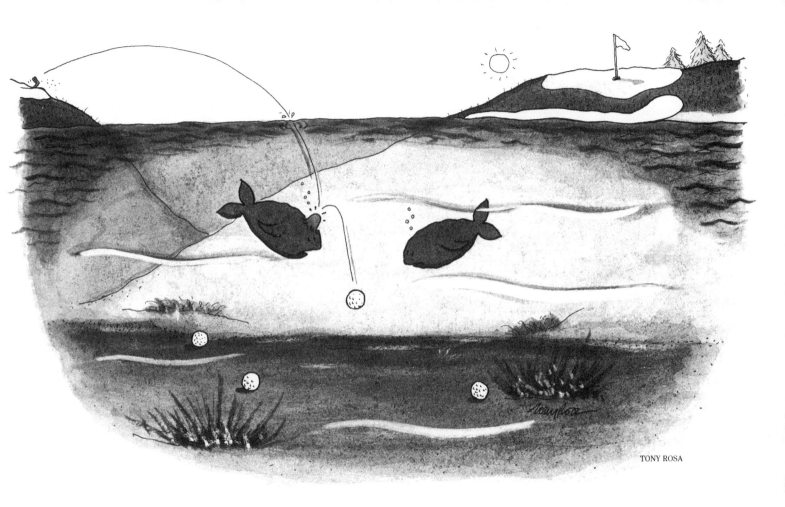

"I miss the fish tank in the clubhouse."

JERRY MARCUS

ED FRASCINO

31

DAVID JACOBSON

"I guess it's that time of year again."

S. GROSS

33

"Nevertheless, I'd feel better if we played a little faster."

JOHN JONIK

35

CHARLES SAUERS

"Someone with our name is winning the U.S. Open!"

HENRY MARTIN

"Do you, Helen, with a handicap of 9, take Clifford, with a handicap of 7 . . . "

BORIS DRUCKER

"I'm trying to raise enough
money to buy my clubs back."

OUT
OF
BOUNDS

JOHN DEMPSEY

LO LINKERT

"The tower says your blind shot out of the woods is no more than three feet from the pin.... The bad news is, the lake's only about *two* feet from the pin."

39

ELI BAUER

MARTY MURPHY

"—Why, yes, Mrs. Feeny—In fact, I have your file in front of me right now."

LEO CULLUM

"Triple bogey."

STEWART
STEWART SLOCUM

WILLIAM MAUL

44

"There's no use wasting the day sulking. Why don't you get out your nice new fountain pen and write some thank-you notes?"

"Amigos, do you mind if the Premier plays through?"

"What makes you so sure he's a hustler?"

"Excuse me. Did you happen to see a 'Patton Penfold' skitter by?"

DON DOUGHTERTY

47

MEL YAUK

1.

2.

3.

JOHN DEMPSEY

"Still too much backswing. Hold your left arm
straighter. Keep your head…"

49

1.

2.

3.

4.

PLOP!

ELI BAUER

50

BILL WOODMAN

The Island of Lost Balls

REVILO

OLIVER CHRISTIANSON (REVILO)

"Look, I'll make you a deal. I'll get my flock to patronize your place if you
get your flock to patronize my place."

53

"He's the only person to pay his membership dues on time."

Woodman

BILL WOODMAN

"What's this I hear about you giving up golf photography?"

Jerry Marcus

JERRY MARCUS

JOHN DEMPSEY

"That's it? 'Keep my head down?'"

"I can't find my life jacket."

"He got up one morning eight years ago and said he was going to take a Mulligan in the game of life. I haven't seen him since."

PORGES

PETER PORGES

Shanahan

DANNY SHANAHAN

"Leave my master alone!"

ARTURO POTTIER

65

BERNARD SCHOENBAUM

"All my life I have wondered about the river Styx. It's roughly about
a five iron, wouldn't you say?"

BRIAN SAVAGE

DICK OLDDEN

"If you knew you had to replace your divots, Herbert, why didn't you do it?"

HARA-KIRI

CHARLES SAUERS

"Where did we go wrong, Alice?"

"It's my husband! Damn! He must have missed the cut!"

MARTY MURPHY

"Internal Revenue Service! Pull over!"

BRIAN SAVAGE

DICK OLDDEN

"Mind if we play through?"

O'NEILL

CATHERINE O'NEILL

75

"I hope we're not going to go through this *every* time you get a hole in one."

DON OREHEK

BRIAN SAVAGE

"You would think that up here, on the last hole, they would let you keep the ball."

79

BILL MAUL

©CASSADY

JOHN CASSADY

"IV!"

"The doctor is going to give you a shot. By the time you wake up, I'll be back."

81

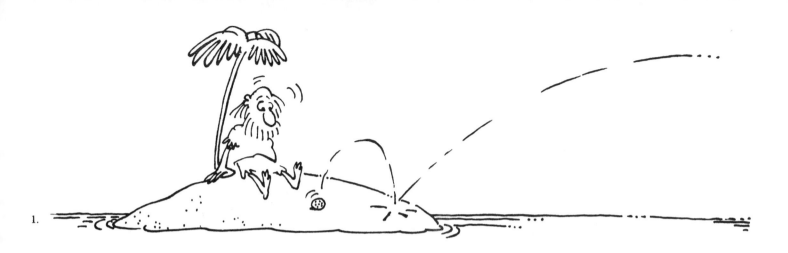

1.

2.

3.

4.

5.

6.

ARAGONÉS
SERGIO ARAGONES

BRIAN SAVAGE

"Yes, it *is* remarkable, I suppose. But the important thing is that he can drop another ball and not be penalized a stroke."

STEWART

STEWART SLOCUM

"Next!"

"Oh, for goodness' sake,
forget it, Beasley. Play
another one."

AARON BACALL

CHARLES SAUERS

86

VAHAN SHIRVANIAN

"Happy birthday. You said you liked to shoot golf."

"You've never kissed me like that!"

CLEM SCALZITTI

88

BRIAN SAVAGE

"I know 217 is a helluva lot for nine holes, Lou, but I also think your caddie left a great deal to be desired."

"That reminds me....Did you pack my golf shoes?"

MARTY MURPHY

89

"Of course I can make a commitment. I'm committed to my job, I'm committed to the Constitution and I'm committed to my golf game."

TONIGHT
GOLFAHOLICS
ANONYMOUS
MEETING
8 PM

JOE MIRACHI

"Thank you, God of Golf!"

AL ROSS

91

BERNARD SCHOENBAUM

ELDON DEDINI

"No matter *how* I treated you, Julia, haunting a man at golf
is hitting below the belt."

BOOK OF WORLD RECORDS

SCHWADRON
HARLEY SCHWADRON

93

CHARLES SAXON

© 1968 The New Yorker Magazine, Inc.

"You're getting cold."

BRIAN SAVAGE

"I thought the Supreme Court outlawed that!"

"What kind of nut would be out fishing in this weather?"

ORLANDO BUSINO

95

"Fore!"

BERNARD SCHOENBAUM

96

AL ROSS

S. GROSS

"Beat it! I don't need a personal demon
when I'm playing golf."

97

AL ROSS

DON OREHEK

"This happens every time we pass the golf course."

LO LINKERT

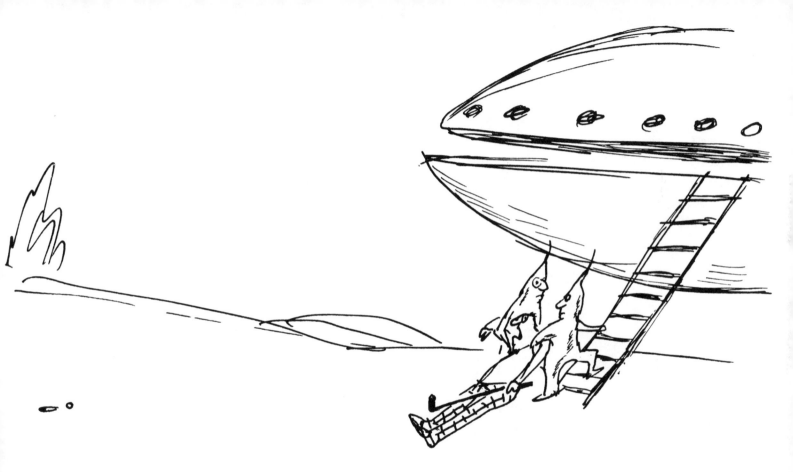

AL ROSS

"*Please*, fellows! For God's sake, let me finish the hole!
I've got an *eagle* coming up!"

101

LO LINKERT

"I'd like golf better if they allowed a designated putter."

ARTEMIS COLE

"I'm on a golf kick. When he mentions golf, I kick him!"

"The roof, please."

JONIK
JOHN JONIK

"The world's greatest invention? I'd say it was those orange golf balls."

GEO LEVINE
GEORGE LEVINE

POLLS

ARTEMIS COLE

"This is for Joan Flaherty. She beat the boss at golf today."

JOHN JONIK

MANNY CURTIS

"It's a rare form of athlete's foot that only golfers get."

S. GROSS

"Remember, son, it isn't whether you win or lose, it's how
you cheat at the game."

NICK DOWNES

"At least you cleared the spent-fuel pond."

CHARLES SAUERS

"Hang in there, Harry—we'll have you out of this
in no time."

MEL YAUK

BRIAN SAVAGE

"I know what you're doing back there, you filthy swine."

DON OREHEK

"I've been here since '81. I hate to think what this has done to my golf game."

JOSEPH FARRIS

109

BRIAN SAVAGE

"Tell me when."

ED FRASCINO

"Fair warning, Randal. I'm this close to becoming
a golf widow for real."

AARON BACALL

"I know it's hard for you to understand how I feel...
but you don't know the course."

ARTEMIS COLE

"You broke 100? Are you on steroids or something?"

BARNEY TOBEY

"Stop *watching* me!"

BILL MAUL

"I've heard of elevated greens before, but this is ridiculous!"

"It says that he found the game of golf inspiring at the expense of it being relaxing."

OLDDEN

DICK OLDDEN

114

OLIVER CHRISTIANSON (REVILO)

115

ALL CADDIES
REPORT IMMEDIATELY
TO THE FIRST TEE!

BRIAN SAVAGE

"I'll look for the ball. You look for the club."

117

"I wouldn't mind her taking that much time putting, but my babysitter costs me a fortune."

LO LINKERT

119

PHIL INTERLANDI

"That's Harry's problem. He's all lessons and no game."

GOLFBALLS THE SIZE OF HAILSTONES

JACK ZIEGLER

"A large bucket of balls and a gag!"

DON OREHEK

"Gosh, Gilliam, it's only golf."